MISSION MINDED

A tool for planning your ministry around Christ's mission

by

Peter Bolt

St Matthias Press

Mission Minded
© St Matthias Press, 1992

St Matthias Press
PO Box 665
LONDON SW20 8RL

ISBN 1 875245 19 7

Typesetting and design by St Matthias Press.

Contents

How to use this book ....5 ✔

1   Mission or maintenance? ....7 ✔

2   Aiming at something biblical ....11 ✔

3   The left-handed game: analysis 19

4   Planning towards mission 29

5   Mission means people 35

6   People mean ministry 43

7   Supporting Christian ministry 47

8   Back to the program 53

9   Over to you! 67

How to use this book

This book is for anyone in ministry, which means it is really for all Christians, since all of us have an obligation to serve others. It contains a simple planning tool which can be used to think about what we're currently doing, what we ought be doing and how to go about it.

Individuals

If you're working through this book on your own to apply it to your own particular ministry, you should find it fairly straightforward. Each chapter (from chapter 2 onwards) shows you a different way to focus your ministry on Christ's mission. You could either:

- work through each of the suggestions as you go, pausing after each chapter to do your own thinking and planning; or
- read the whole book through quickly to get an idea of how it all works and then come back and work through each phase more slowly.

Groups

The tool is also extremely valuable for groups, such as church committees, parish councils, leadership teams, and so on. You could work through the chapters at a series of regular meetings, or you could go away together for a few days and do it intensively. The best method would probably be to read each chapter privately, in advance, and then get together to discuss its content and to work through the implications for your ministry.

1

Mission or maintenance?

Are you involved in Mission or Maintenance? What a question! How do you know? And who wants to answer it anyway? The way the question is often put makes it clear that you take a risk if you answer it. Your answer will firmly place you in only one of two groups—it will place you amongst the real movers who are going somewhere and taking their group of Christians with them, or it will reveal that you are part of the vast mass of Christian leaders who have supposedly renounced that title in practice, are going nowhere and taking no-one with them! So what does the question do for you? Does it bring on cold sweats, as you feel your whole life and ministry and self-esteem threatened? Or does it give you a touch of Pharisaic pride, seeing that you know you are on the right track and can revel in the answer you have been invited to spout about?

These two M-words seem to have become a new dividing stick amongst Christians, and a new way to evaluate a minister's work. Recently I heard of one group of people on the prowl for a new pastor who bewailed the fact that 95% of the people they interviewed were in 'Maintenance Mode' not 'Mission Mode'. It almost sounds like two competing Christian fashion magazines. This group were after a

'Mission Minded' not 'Maintenance Minded' pastor, and so they hadn't, at that time, found someone for their charge. We can only speculate about the 95% they left behind: did this group of concerned pastor-seekers inform the rejected clergy of their ailment, and what happened when they did? Were the Maintenance men hard-liners who had chosen to be 'Self-consciously Maintenance Minded', were proud of it, and glad to see the backs of these Mission Seeking Morons! Or were they 'Accidently Maintenance Minded', somehow not noticing that they had left their Mission behind until this group of nouveau Pharisees kindly informed them that they hadn't met the standards of this new law? Or were they 'Occasionally Maintenance Minded', vacillating between moments of Mission and moments of Maintenance, and unfortunately happened to be wallowing in the latter when they were visited by the 'Mission Mafia'? Were they left in their studieswondering where they went wrong?

Alternatives?

Of course, there *is* a point to the distinction, even if it shouldn't be used against fellow Christians for whom Christ died. Every Christian is drafted into Christ's Mission as soon as they are converted. The Son of Man came to seek and to save the lost (Lk 19:10), and on the latter side of his death and resurrection his people are to carry on this task until he returns. To follow Jesus as his disciple means to be unashamed of him *and his words*, being prepared to suffer for his sake *and for the sake of his gospel* (Mk 8:35, 38). It is a usual reaction for converted people to want to "proclaim the excellencies of him who called you out of darkness into his marvellous light" (1 Pet 2:9), and as soon as you open your mouth you step into the Mission. Mission is clearly the priority for individual Christians, and for groups of Christians, for it is the priority of our Lord and our God.

Then there is Maintenance. In the Mafia's vocabulary this is clearly on the down-side. They mean by this term 'simply maintaining the status quo', long after the reason for that 'quo' has been lost or outdated or forgotten or brutally murdered. So whatever gets started keeps going on and on and on and on. Nothing ever changes; this year is the same as last year, and the year before that. The only reason for doing anything is that 'We've always done it that way'. The only reason needed to *not* do something is that 'We've never done it that way'. This kind of Maintenance smells very much like the traditions of men that get in the way of the real things of God's Kingdom (Mk 7:5-8), and it sounds very close to the man-made religious practices that God hated in the Old Testament and that Jesus and the apostles attacked in the New. What Christian wants that? And what Christian leader wants to be leading in that direction? Such Maintenance is rightly despised.

But the confusing thing is that there is a right kind of Maintenance. Isn't it right to nurture people's faith, maintain their Christian walk, keep them persevering to the end, and all that? Don't some of the things already going on in the church help maintain such good directions? Why should they be changed just to avoid the slanders of the Mission Mafia? Of course there is a place for maintaining the status quo—as long as the status quo still serves a useful purpose in furthering Christ's Mission to a lost world. That is the key.

Another problem is that we can all get in a rut. Despite good intentions and commitments to stay in 'Mission Mode', the pressures and busyness of normal twentieth century life combined with the pressures and busyness of normal twentieth century Christian ministry, seem to drag us towards a 'Maintenance Mentality'. It is far easier to stay with what we've got. And it is just plain hard work to get something new up and running. It is a breeze to do whatever others thrust upon you, but a stormy process indeed to think of what you would like to thrust upon them. It makes you so acceptable to others when you respond to their needs, rather than saying 'No' to them so you can pursue your own agenda on their behalf. Scratching people where they say they have an itch pleases everyone—everyone, that is, except that confounded Mission Mafia! They persist in shaking their heads in your direction and whispering to each other behind their hands.

To save face with this group, what can we do? But the issue is more important than that, isn't it? To help overcome the natural drag away from Mission, what can we do? For Christ's Mission is about saving the lost. Without Christ, people are utterly lost. With Christ they are utterly found; they are utterly saved. It is therefore of the utmost importance to be involved in his Mission, and to maintain only those things that further his Mission. The question is, how can we do it?

Where are the posts?

Part of the answer involves setting goals. But we can set goals about anything and everything—just setting goals is not the thing. Our goals ought to be *Mission* goals, and these Mission goals ought then to govern our ministry. That *doesn't* mean that there will be no Maintenance, but it *does* mean that Maintenance will be justified according to the Mission goals, like anything else that gets included in our ministry.

Mission goals will consist of some fairly general things that will always be a part of any Christian ministry, for these things are determined by the Bible. People will always need to be evangelized; Christians will always need to be edified in their faith and equipped for Christian service (Eph 4:12); faithful people will always need to be freed up to teach other faithful people to teach other faithful people to... (2 Tim 2:2). Such general and necessary goals may take different specific forms in various places and at various times, or to various types of people. But no matter what specific form they may take, they are plainly drawn from God's Word and should therefore govern everything else.

What follows is a simple tool. It is not 'Everything you wanted to know about ministry, but were afraid to ask'. It will not give you all the answers to becoming Mission Minded about ministry—I hope I'm not that big-headed. It will also need further refinement from you as you use it in the specific context of your ministry. But it is a tool that will help you think through your ministry in a way that is governed by Mission goals.

It is a tool that will be useful to anyone engaged in Christian ministry. And that means you—for all Christians are involved in ministry (Eph 4:12). It is helpful for:

- ministry one-to-one
- churches setting up new ministries
- churches analysing their old ministries
- anyone with some leadership role in a structured ministry situation such as a Sunday School Class, a youth group or an Adult Bible Study
- a pastor who has oversight of all the ministries in a church

Without further ado, let's take a look at it. Who knows, you may have it mastered before the Mission Mafia next comes knocking on your door!

Aiming at something biblical

The tool to help resurrect us from Maintenance to that far more acceptable 'M' is extremely simple. It has to be. Who wants something that is so complex that no-one even knows which way is up?

The tool consists of a piece of paper. That's right, an ordinary piece of paper—any colour, practically any size, and it doesn't matter if it has a Bible verse along the bottom or not. Along the top of the paper are listed several very general goals that are drawn from the Bible. Several? Okay, basically it is only two, but they are subdivided so that the tool doesn't look *too* basic (we have our pride, don't we?). Two? Well, there is also an additional 'supportive goal' which I'll mention later. Under these goals we have columns drawn and, to the far left, we have a column that is blank for the moment. In the following chapters we will discover that the contents of this left-hand column are variable, depending upon how the tool is being applied. Here is a diagram, so that we are all picturing the same thing right at the beginning:

Variable left-hand column	GOAL 1 Subgoals			GOAL 2 Subgoals			Supportive Goal

There are two goals that every Christian involved in ministry ought to adopt. These general goals form the basis of this mission tool.

1.   Evangelism

The first is evangelism. God's chosen way of bringing people into his Kingdom is through the proclamation of the gospel of Christ. As men and women hear of Christ's death and resurrection on their behalf, and his present reign as Lord before his promised return, and they believe, so they enter into God's Kingdom. Such people then experience the joy of forgiveness of sins, the certainty of eternal life, and the freedom of Christian discipleship in fellowship with other believers. But the entry point is the proclamation of the gospel. Whenever the gospel is proclaimed, that is evangelism. Therefore, part of our Mission goals must be that Jesus' name is proclaimed as the only way of salvation. "Salvation is found in no-one else, for there is no other name under heaven given to men by which we must be saved" (Acts 4:12). In another place, Paul says: "For how can they call on the one they have not believed in? And how can they believe in the one of whom they have not heard? And how can they hear without someone preaching to them? And how can they preach unless they are sent?" (Rom 10:14–15). When he says this, he is making the point that Israel in fact *received* the necessary preaching and still refused to believe. But, for our purposes, we simply need to notice the logical questions that he asks in the course of his argument. Evangelism is necessary for anyone to hear about Jesus and so believe and be saved. Evangelism is the proclamation of the gospel. This proclamation needs to be done by somebody.

Before a person can hear the gospel they need to be in contact with a gospel preacher, that is, a Christian. It is God's chosen method that he sends preachers of the gospel to others. I guess he could have done it some other way if he had chosen to do so, but the fact is, he didn't. Evangelism is done by people to people for people. This then gives us a sub-goal: there must be contact between the Christian (the gospel preacher) and the one who needs to hear the gospel. Christians need to be in contact with people so that they can take the opportunities that God will provide for gospel proclamation.

Now, a lot of people cross our path in the course of normal life: neighbours, workmates, family and friends; other people's neighbours, workmates, family, and friends; visitors to church, casual acquaintances, etc. These people have contact with a Christian by virtue of these relationships. But there are other people who never come into contact with a Christian in the normal course of life. How can these people hear the gospel? Surely they must somehow be reached as well. This gives us another sub-goal: We ought to attempt to raise people's awareness of the gospel or Christians or our church, in the hope of making contact with them in the future.

It also seems fairly common that people are in contact with a Christian for some time before an opportunity for evangelism is taken by the Christian. This period of time can be called 'pre-evangelism'. Certainly the Christian ought to be praying for opportunities to share the gospel so that the relationship is heading towards evangelism. However, until the gospel is actually proclaimed it is not evangelism, just pre-evangelism.

So, under our first main goal of Evangelism we have ended up with four sub-goals, all heading towards the proclamation of the gospel to a non-Christian. These can be set out as follows, with an arrow to indicate the desired direction of movement:

Variable left-hand column	GOAL 1 = EVANGELISM				GOAL 2
	Raising Awareness	Initial Contact	Pre-Evangelism	Evangelism	
	➡	➡	➡	➡	

13

2. Edification

The second major goal is Edification. It is God's desire that all of his people are conformed more and more to the likeness of Jesus Christ. Edification is the building up of Christians into this likeness. Of course, this will only be completed on the Last Day, but it is the present aim of every Christian's life to progress towards the maturity that will be theirs on that Last Day.

This goal can also be broken down. When people are first converted to Christ, it is always beneficial to give them some special treatment, some basic 'follow-up'. It seems that the apostle Paul was keen to do this with the Thessalonians, since he writes to them and also sends Timothy to find out about their faith (1 Thess 3:1-5). In fact, a good case can be made that it was his constant practice to 'follow-up' new believers.

But the need for edification never stops, for when it ceases we will have arrived in heaven. (And does it stop there? I'll wait and see!) Until that day, all Christians need to be 'nurtured' in their Christian life.

Two further sub-goals can now be added to the tool:

Variable left-hand column	EVANGELISM				EDIFICATION				Supportive Goal
	Raising Awareness	Initial Contact	Pre-Evangelism	Evangelism	Follow-up	Nurture			

But there is more to the Christian life than being followed-up and nurtured. If that was all, we would not be too different from the Pharisees who were so scrupulously concerned about their own piety. This self-centred religion may be the natural default state of every human heart, but Christ's followers know that this is not true religion. Christ, in his mercy, has given each Christian a 'work of service', a ministry, to be engaged in for the sake of his body, the church (Eph 4:11-12). His aim in doing so was that the church might be edified. In other words, it is not just individual Christians that need building up, but the whole of Christ's church. His purposes are far wider than this individual or that individual; he is creating a whole new people for himself. And it is as "...each part does its work" that the "...whole body...grows and builds itself up in love" (Eph 4:16).

Within Christ's church, some people have a special kind of ministry. Those people who bring God's word to the rest of the church have been given to the church so that all ministries will be developed and nurtured. "(Christ) gave some to be apostles, some to be prophets, some to be evangelists, and some as pastors/teachers, to prepare God's people for their works of service, so that the body of Christ may be built up" (Eph 4:11-12). These people are to train and equip Christians, by the explanation of God's word, for their works of service (their 'ministries').

This enables another sub-goal to be formulated. As soon as you have Christians, you have people who ought to be engaged in and trained for ministry for the greater benefit of Christ's body, the church. Therefore we ought to aim at training Christians for ministry. Our tool is now getting wider:

Variable left–hand column	EVANGELISM				EDIFICATION			Supportive Goal
	Raising Awareness	Initial Contact	Pre–Evangelism	Evangelism	Follow-up	Nurture	Training in Ministry	

3. Support to Ministry

There is one more goal to be added to our basic tool. It is in its own category, which we can call 'support to ministry'. Now, I know that whatever ministry a Christian is involved in could be called ministry in the full sense. But it will be seen below that it is useful to separate Ministry proper—i.e. the activities that have some specific role in either getting the gospel to people or growing the church—and those activities that *support* this ministry. Perhaps this category is close to what the Bible calls the gift of administration or 'helps' (1 Cor 12:28). This category will be further clarified when examples are given in Chapter 7.

The basic tool has now been constructed. To enable us to set Mission goals for our ministry, certain general goals can be drawn from the Bible and slightly sub-divided to give us the following:

Variable left-hand column	EVANGELISM				EDIFICATION			SUPPORT TO MINISTRY
	Raising Awareness	Initial Contact	Pre-Evangelism	Evangelism	Follow-up	Nurture	Training in Ministry	Support to Ministry

Now that the goals and subgoals are listed across our page, we are almost ready to turn to the most important left-hand variable column. But before we do, let's take a look at these goals again. As we do so, it becomes apparent that there is a progression from left to right. Take Mr. Average Unbeliever. He starts out totally unaware that anything Christian even exists. He thinks churches are old electricity substations, or funeral homes modelled on St Pancras station in London. He thinks being religious means never ever missing the Friday after-work session at the pub. What does he need? He needs Column One: he needs to have his awareness of Christianity raised. Then he may come across a Christian. Column Two has been filled: Initial Contact. Say he then gets to know this Christian for some time—Column Three: Pre-evangelism. Then, eventually, the Christian (who has been praying for opportunities to share the gospel with Mr Average) asks him if he knows anything about Jesus Christ and eternal life and all that stuff. He doesn't, so the Christian asks whether he'd mind if he let him have it. He doesn't, so he does—Column Four: Evangelism. Mr Average reckons it is the best news he's heard since last year's Christmas bonus, so he believes it and becomes a Christian. His new brother, a truly amazing specimen, decides to meet with him weekly to help him understand the new life he has just received—Column Five: Follow-Up. Lo and behold, Mr Average-Ex-Unbeliever begins at church and Bible study—Column Six: Nurture. After a while he wants to learn how to share the gospel with others who are still like he used to be, so he joins a Personal Evangelism course at the local church hall— Column Seven: Training in Ministry. And sometime during the whole process he realises that he can give some of his money to enable other people to hear the good news that he has heard—Column Eight: Support to Ministry.

Of course, not everyone moves through all these stages, and it certainly isn't strictly chronological. In fact, many things may be going on at the same time and people may cross from one column to the next without any show of emotion whatsoever! But we can still say that there is a loose progression from left to right on the page.

Now that we have the top of the page all set up, what happens down the left-hand side?

3

The left-handed game: analysis

T he left-hand column varies according to how the tool is used. The following chapters will outline these uses by suggesting various left-hand columns.

Since we have all but admitted that we are already engaged in ministry but probably in Maintenance Mode (at least sometimes, if only because we really don't know how to recognize this problem), why don't we begin with what we've already got. To use that expression that has become a cliche, let's use the tool to see *where we are coming from*. The tool is extremely useful for *analysis*.

For example, let's say you are a pastor who arrives in a church knowing very little about it (as distinct from a pastor who *leaves* a church knowing very little about it!). Changing cliches slightly, you want to assess *where the church is at*. Get out your paper, draw up the goals and their underlying columns and leave your hand poised over the vacant left-hand column. If it makes you feel like you are getting somewhere you can even write at its head 'Analysis', or 'St Bob's' plus the date, or even 'Analysis of St Bob's as at' plus the date, if you want to be absolutely precise-verging-on-overkill.

Then, on a new line each time, list out totally at random all the

ANALYSIS OF ST BOB'S

ACTIVITY	EVANGELISM				EDIFICATION		
	Raising Awareness	Initial Contact	Pre-Evangelism	Evangelism	Follow-up	Nurture	Training in Ministry
Sunday Church							
Agnostics Anonymous							
C E Follow-up							
Craft groups							
Bible study							
Playgroups							
Sunday School							
Scripture							
Youth groups							
Creche							
Baptismal visits							
Doorknocking							
Hiring ministry trainee							
Bookstall							
Golf day							
Marriages							
Funerals							
Family nights							
Family Sundays							
Lord's supper							
Leafletting							
Hospitality							
Sidespeople							
Welcoming							
Ladies coffee morning							
Working bee							
Committee							
Rosters							
Minister							
Prayer meeting							
Morning tea							

activities that you know the church is involved in. List everything and anything, no matter how big or small. You ought to get a page like the one opposite (only with your church's activities on it).

For your next step, think about each activity in turn. Ask yourself: What is the major function of this activity, in terms of the goals and sub-goals at the top of the page? It may even be helpful to talk to the people involved in the activity to gain their perception of what they think they are trying to achieve by their group/activity. (There may be a discrepancy between what people perceive the function to be and what you feel it ought to be, but this process should enable clarification as well as analysis for its own sake. Another use for the tool: better communication!) As you arrive at the main function, put a dark box in the relevant column. So, for example, you may discover that the annual 'Guest Service' is not simply so you can have a guest speaker to give the pastor a day off, but that it is designed for congregation members to bring their own guests to hear the gospel explained, and to be invited to make a decision to follow Christ and be saved. In other words it falls under the main aim Evangelism. Your table will therefore look like this:

	EVANGELISM				EDIFICATION		
ACTIVITY	Raising Awareness	Initial Contact	Pre-Evangelism	Evangelism	Follow-up	Nurture	Training in Ministry
Guest Service				▨			

However, some activities may not be this simple to categorise. You may find that some activities have a number of functions, or the people involved in them may not agree on what the main function is meant to be. Well, at this stage it does not matter too much, for you are still analysing what you *have* got, rather than planning what you *should* have got. Later on you may want to clarify or change the main function, but for the time being use dotted lines for what you perceive to be secondary functions, still trying to identify a main function with a dark box.

An example will help. A lady in the church has a monthly meeting in her home to which she invites her neighbours for coffee and some other activity. The other activity is usually something that is relevant for the type of person in the area, e.g. a talk on child rearing, a cooking demonstration, a craft thing, etc. The woman sees that this type of activity helps her to get to know non-Christian ladies, with the hope and prayer that an opportunity to share the gospel will arise. All of this puts the activity in the 'Pre-Evangelism' column. However, at a couple of occasions in the year, you learn that someone is invited to talk about the gospel. For instance, last year someone spoke on the meaning of Christmas, and someone else gave a talk on Easter and answered questions about Christianity. Since these activities specifically involve the proclamation of the gospel, they are Evangelism. This means that this monthly meeting functions mainly as Pre-Evangelism, but occasionally as Evangelism, and so the diagram ends up like this:

	EVANGELISM				EDIFICATION		
ACTIVITY	Raising Awareness	Initial Contact	Pre-Evangelism	Evangelism	Follow-up	Nurture	Training in Ministry
Ladies Coffee Morning			�				

It may get even more complicated. You know an older guy who loves knocking on doors and telling people that there is a church down the road at which they would be most welcome (you have already checked, he does mean yours!) and which wants to be of any service to the community that they can be. Okay, this activity fits into 'Initial Contact'. (It isn't 'Raising Awareness' because it involves a non-Christian actually coming into personal contact with a Christian). But then, as you talk to this guy, you also find out that he loves taking someone with him on his visits, because he feels that they will benefit from the experience and be more confident about sharing their own faith some day. That means that he has the aim of training someone else for ministry. Now your diagram has a box in two columns that are not next to each other—it may not be neat, but it is certainly informative:

	EVANGELISM				EDIFICATION		
ACTIVITY	Raising Awareness	Initial Contact	Pre-Evangelism	Evangelism	Follow-up	Nurture	Training in Ministry
Doorknock		�					⬚

Doing such thinking about every activity you have listed will be hard, but it will be most worthwhile. When you have finished, you will immediately see where the focus of your church lies—whether there is a spread of activities across all goals, or whether there is some imbalance.

If there are a lot of dotted lines, it means that there are a lot of activities with unclear goals and more clarification is needed. A church with this analysis needs to work out what they are trying to achieve!

	EVANGELISM				EDIFICATION		
ACTIVITY	Raising Awareness	Initial Contact	Pre-Evangelism	Evangelism	Follow-up	Nurture	Training in Ministry
Doorknocking	⬚	⬚					
Baptismal inquiries		⬚---⬚					
Guest services		⬚------------⬚					
Church		⬚------------------------------⬚					

The old proverb says that if you aim at nothing you are sure to hit it. It seems equally true that if you aim at everything you are sure to hit just as much as if you aimed at nothing! My guess is that this church would have quite a lot of furious activity that is achieving very little because, quite simply, it is aiming at too little by trying to aim at everything with every activity! Activities with a clearly defined function will be more productive in the long run.

Are there heaps of boxes in one column? Like these:

ACTIVITY	EVANGELISM				EDIFICATION		
	Raising Awareness	Initial Contact	Pre-Evangelism	Evangelism	Follow-up	Nurture	Training in Ministry
Coffee morning			▭				
Men's mechanics night			▭				
Men's golf day			▭				
Bush dance			▭				
Carols by Candlelight			▭				

ACTIVITY	EVANGELISM				EDIFICATION		
	Raising Awareness	Initial Contact	Pre-Evangelism	Evangelism	Follow-up	Nurture	Training in Ministry
Morning church						▭	
Evening church						▭	
Bible study						▭	
Input day						▭	
Correspondence Course group						▭	

The problem with the first, is that all the pre-evangelism in the world won't get anyone converted. Something must be done in the evangelism column—and fast.

With the second, the 'saints' are getting well fed—engorged, in fact—but what about 'the sinners'? This profile suggests that this much-edified church has lost sight of the Mission and, rather than taking the gospel to the nations (like Matt 28:18-20 mentions), it has become introverted. Something must be done in the evangelism column—and fast.

The same problem, looked at in another way, would arise if some goals lacked any boxes in their columns. For example, this church:

ACTIVITY	EVANGELISM				EDIFICATION		
	Raising Awareness	Initial Contact	Pre-Evangelism	Evangelism	Follow-up	Nurture	Training in Ministry
Ladies Coffee morning			▓	�			
Christianity Explained				▓			
Doorknock Evangelism Explosion		▓		▓			▓
Trained Nurturer's					▓		
Bible study						▓	

This church needs to decide whether they wish to 'raise awareness' more in their community, perhaps through a catchy ad in the local paper, or a 'sandwich board' on the nearby busy road, or a letter box drop, or whatever.

25

Or this church:

ACTIVITY	EVANGELISM				EDIFICATION		
	Raising Awareness	Initial Contact	Pre-Evangelism	Evangelism	Follow-up	Nurture	Training in Ministry
Church				▨		▨	
Guest Services				▨			
Evangelism Explosion				▨			▨
Newspaper ad	▨						
Coffee morning			▨ ▭				
Sign on highway	▨						

They obviously have a lot of evangelistic activities set up, but with nothing aiming at 'initial contact' they may find that eventually they have no-one to evangelize any more. This may lead to some plans to begin to rub shoulders with a new bunch of non-Christians: a doorknock perhaps; or a strategy to visit some institution like a prison, or a hospital, or an office block, or a place of education; a questionnaire at the railway station in the afternoon rush; a plan to encourage congregation members to join a sporting club, or to hold a summer street party, or a post-election BBQ.

If there are columns with nothing in them, it doesn't necessarily mean that something *must* be put into that column immediately. Sometimes it *does* mean this. For example, if there is no direct evangelism going on, or any edification of the believers, something is seriously amiss and the situation needs to be rectified *now*. But some activities may not be as crucial. A church may be doing nothing specifically to 'raise awareness', but may still have a flood of people turning up to the church, being evangelized and so on. It might be perfectly appropriate to leave that column blank for the time being. However, a blank column certainly means that the situation needs to be assessed. If it is left blank, it should be done so after some hard thinking, and after a commitment to re-assess this decision when circumstances change.

We have now strayed beyond simple analysis, which is where we began. But that is not a bad thing, for it is the step that follows naturally. So why don't we turn to this next use of the tool: Planning.

4

Planning towards mission

O nce you have analysed your (occasionally/usually/constantly/ eternally—strike out whatever is inapplicable) maintenance-oriented church, if you still have the energy you no doubt want to ask a very simple question: 'What next?'. I'm glad you asked. 'What next' is to do some planning that will take you closer towards mission. This may be done by the pastor; it may be done by a committee; but the important thing is that it is done!

As mentioned in the last chapter, the analysis may have revealed certain imbalances in the church's activities. Let's say, for example, that there was a whole host of things in the Pre-Evangelism column, and absolutely nothing in the Evangelism column. This could easily happen, because it is easy to confuse the two. You see, Christians have a heart for getting people converted and so they have an evangelistic *desire*. This desire can result in all kinds of activities which are set up in great hope that they will get people converted. But the fact is that often there is *no specific plan to verbally share the gospel, and it is this verbal sharing of the gospel that is evangelism.* No matter how much evangelistic desire we have, unless the gospel is shared the activity is Pre-Evangelism not Evangelism. But when there is a lot of evangelistic desire there are bound to be a lot of activities that have sprung out of that desire, and so, almost without noticing it, a church can generate many items which ought to be properly labelled Pre-Evangelism, sometimes to the neglect of Evangelism itself.

ACTIVITY	EVANGELISM				EDIFICATION		
	Raising Awareness	Initial Contact	Pre-Evangelism	Evangelism	Follow-up	Nurture	Training in Ministry
Coffee morning			▭				
Men's mechanics night			▭				
Men's golf day			▭				
Barn dance			▭				
Carols by Candelight			▭				

This church needs to recognise that this situation is not good (for nobody will get converted if the gospel is not shared—that is just a fact of life), and then decide what can be done to rectify the situation. Through reflection on the Bible, they realise that the solution consists of proclaiming the gospel, for it is *the gospel* that is the power of God for salvation to everyone who believes (Rom 1:16)—not the young mums' playgroup, no matter how excellently it is run! So the planners must take this into account and plan something that will give this church an evangelistic edge.

However, although there must always be something in the Evangelism column, there may be certain other deficits that are deemed acceptable, given the stage of life the church is at. For instance, the 'Raising Awareness' column may be very thin. Its only representative may be that the church building has a sign out front and is located on a reasonably major road. Other activities may be canvassed to fill this lack (advertising in the local paper, a letterbox drop, beer mats in the local pub with the service times on them, a banner behind a plane on Cup Final Day!), but all of them require more money than you have to spend. As well as this, there are heaps of people already in contact with the church people through the multitude of Pre-Evangelistic activities, so the need to raise awareness is not so urgent at this stage. The decision can be legitimately made not to do anything about this lack now, but it will be reviewed when circumstances change.

On the other hand, the analysis may actually force you to consider whether there are too many activities in the Pre-Evangelism column. Perhaps these activities are demanding lots of time and energy and maybe also money. Perhaps you have noticed that it is fairly hard to maintain the motivation of the Christians who are involved, for they seem to put in so much but see so little fruit for their effort: "Nobody seems to be getting converted and we've been at it for so long now". Perhaps it is time to prune some of these Pre-Evangelistic activities (which will never get anyone converted without some specific evangelism) and institute some specific Evangelism. Once this decision is made, what happens then?

Target Groups

Here is another use for the tool. Whenever an activity is listed in the left-hand column, it is very helpful to also list its 'Target Group' as clearly as possible. For instance, a playgroup is by its very nature aimed at non-working mothers with pre-school children. (If in doubt about who the target group actually is, go along to the activity and ask yourself, what do all these people have in common? That question will begin to provide some answers.)

However, you may notice that your church has three playgroups running. A mistake for the young player in the ministry analysis game would be to decide immediately to axe two of the groups, in the interests of cleaning out the Pre-Evangelism column. After all, they all have the same label ('Playgroup'), and it seems inefficient to have three, and oh-so-neat to have only one group assigned to each label. But this is definitely a trap, and the seasoned campaigner will be wise to it. The fact is that a church might have several playgroups running on different days or at different times which are suitable for different people. They may draw mothers from different geographical locations, since neighbours tend to bring neighbours along. They might draw mothers from different sociological groups, since the single mum on state benefit can't afford to keep up with the dress standards of the 'twin-set and pearls' group of mums that attend playgroup after their tennis morning. So, even though you may have three 'Playgroups' listed in your left-hand column, when target groups are analysed more closely you end up with:

| Playgroup: Non-working on Tuesday Morning mothers from area A. |
| Playgroup: Non-working on Thursday Morning mothers from area B. |
| Playgroup: Non-working on Friday Morning mothers from areas A & B. |

A check on the attendance also confirms that there are three distinct groups of women coming along. Conclusion: these are three distinct activities under the aim of Pre-Evangelism. If there is no other good reason to stop one or more of these, then it would be a mistake to wield the razor just because the Pre-Evangelism column looked too full. They all seem to be performing a useful function and they are not overlapping at all.

However, the target group analysis may reveal that this is not the case with some other activities. You may find that the craft group, the women's guild, the Friday coffee morning and the monthly women's Saturday get together all have as their target group women in the 40-50 year age bracket. A check on rolls also reveals that the ten or twelve ladies in that bracket attend all of these groups. Not only that, but each group is run by a different person in the church, so there seems to be an obvious waste of human resources upon this small group of ladies. Conclusion: a decision needs to be made about whether some pruning needs to occur within *this particular set* of Pre-Evangelistic activities.

Target groups are an excellent way to structure the planning of a church's activities, even beyond the help it provides in analysis. In the left-hand column, activities can be grouped according to their target. Churches usually have age-related groups, and often sex-type related groups, which could give a left-hand column as follows:

Pre-schoolers						
Creche (9am Sunday)						
Playgroups						
School-age (Primary)						
Tuesday Kids Club						
Sunday School						
Secondary School						
Friday Fellowship						
Adult (Men)						
Men's BBQ quarterly						
Adult (Women)						
Women's Bible Study						

Listing out the functions performed by each group can then enable the planning of where and how each person in that age group is being evangelized, edified or trained in ministry.

But it can go further than just the groups traditionally run by churches (we don't want to wallow in 'Maintenance Mode' any longer, do we?!). Now we are on the way to Mission, we want to think beyond the activities we already have. The tool can help us to do this. If the left-hand column is given to the target groups we wish to reach, then the remainder of the columns can be filled in as we plan how each group is to be contacted, evangelized, edified, etc.

Another example: suppose your area has had a big influx of a certain racial group which you feel needs to be reached for the gospel. List this group in the left-hand column, then go across the other goals and plan how you will raise awareness, contact and evangelize *this particular group*. Or suppose you notice there are no teenagers in your church, and yet everywhere you look in the suburb they are crawling up the lamp-posts and sliding around street corners, and you decide they are a group that needs to be reached. What do you do? Put them in the left-hand column and then plan each step through the other columns. Your page may end up something like this:

Once such planning is done, you should have a fairly comprehensive diagram across your piece of (was it blue?) paper—your 'Mission Minded' tool. At a glance in the left-hand column you can see the activity and the target group. Reading across the columns you can see what activities perform what functions, now hopefully in dark boxes rather than dotted ones. (Although some will always have a blurred or multiple function, most should have a clearly defined aim—it helps to know what you are trying to hit!) This will be an extremely useful document. Guard it with your life!

Such a document will enable the groups to know clearly who they are trying to reach, and what they are trying to achieve with these people. That will help them do it. It will also enable the right people to be invited to the right activity. And that is the heart of ministry, isn't it? For isn't ministry about a particular kind of service to a particular kind of person with a specific kind of need? That is what we ought to turn to right now. But it can wait until chapter 5, if you insist.

Mission means people

Ministry is really quite simple, even though, as with anything, we simple people have a tendency to make the simple things too complex to handle. But ministry is simple, at least in its basics. For isn't ministry about three P's? It is about **Proclamation**—telling people about Jesus, preaching the gospel, evangelizing people. It is about **Prayer**—asking God to work through his word, like he promises to do. It is about **People**—loving them, caring enough about them to speak the truth of God's word to them, whether it is convenient or inconvenient for them. **P**roclaiming, **P**raying, **P**eople-ing: that is Christian ministry.

Now, the trouble with being susceptible to Maintenance Mode, is that we too easily get stuck in the rut of simply maintaining 'structures'. That is, we run groups and activities and programs and meetings and more meetings. Now, all of that sounds very different to the three P's, doesn't it? And let me assure you, all of that is nowhere near as exciting as being involved in real Christian ministry! And let me tell you another thing, the reason it is not nearly so exciting is that God doesn't promise to work through 'meetings' and he very rarely does! God promises to work through his Word (proclamation), in response to our requests (prayers) for John, Mary, Minh Tan, Xerxes and Abdul (people)—and he actually does! And that is what makes Christian ministry exciting.

It doesn't help us either when so much of the world's understanding of Christianity is far from the real thing. Many people—both church people and non-church people—define Christianity *organizationally* ('What's the official line on...') or *formally* (as if it is only about church services on Sunday). It is very easy for pastors to begin to see themselves merely as people who function in a certain role that is prescribed by the community around them or the expectations of the people in their local congregation or, worse still, their distant denomination. They begin to 'do a job', like any other person, except it is 'The Ministry'. They can even be heard to talk as if they had a career path within their organisation (read 'denomination'), and some have even talked of 'job satisfaction'. Yuk! But all of that is the maintenance rut that is so easy to slip into. Ministry is service of Christ in his mission to a lost world. And this kind of ministry—real ministry—is simply proclamation, prayer and people.

So far we have applied the tool to analysing and planning the structures of a church. I began at this end because, if we really are in the maintenance rut, that is exactly what we think ministry is! If we are wallowing down there—either permanently or just momentarily—we will envisage ministry in terms of what activities and groups and programs our church is involved in. Well, the tool is a help for all these things, and they all do have their place and so we have begun with these things.

However, if ministry is about people, we have to move on to another way of thinking and another use of the tool, perhaps an even more important use. Another cliche of the Mission Mafia is that ministry is 'people not programs'—keep that one under your belt for when they next turn up! (If you drop it in conversation it earns at least 10 extra points on the 'Good Guy' list.) Programs do have their place, but they must never be allowed to eclipse the fact that we care about people: people who are lost *without* Christ; people who are found for eternity *with* Christ. That is why we must move on to a further use of this tool.

But let's get there slowly. Why rush things? Let's rejoin our newly arrived pastor. He has analysed the structures of the church, and done some planning so that he now knows what the church structures are aiming to do and who they are aiming to do it to. Now, how does he 'get people involved'?

'Getting people involved'

A common method is the smorgasbord approach. Don't get me wrong, I like the smorgasbord approach—but in restaurants, not in churches. In the right place, it is great to be offered everything and have the freedom to eat what you like, when you like—which usually means everything, and all night! But in churches this doesn't seem to be the way to go. What usually happens is that we offer everyone everything and they end up with indigestion as a result.

For example, if we do a leaflet drop, why list every conceivable activity that the church has going and tell them that they are welcome to anything and everything they like? If someone gets converted and is really keen, why make sure that they are involved in everything that is going? Is it because we have to nab them while their initial keenness lasts? If there is a church activity, why is it an unwritten eleventh commandment that the whole church must be involved? Is it because we feel it is a threat to unity if every single member doesn't turn up?

But our newly arrived pastor knows better. Now that he clearly knows what each activity is trying to achieve, he will invite people to be involved in *only what is relevant for them*. Are they non-Christian? He looks down his Evangelism column and invites them to the 'Christianity Explained' course. Are they Christian but needing to know the basics? He looks down his Edification columns before hitting them with the idea of some personal follow-up, spilling into one of the Bible Study groups. Are they involved in a pre-evangelistic activity? Well, he would never even think of inviting them to another such activity; he will ask them to something evangelistic next.

Principles

There are a number of principles which operate once the activities of a church are itemized and analysed. Remember that the movement is towards the right. Therefore, that is the direction of invitations as well. If someone is already contacted, he doesn't need to be made aware. If they are converted they don't need to be evangelized for the first time! *The invitation ought to be towards the right, not the left.* That is principlenumber one.

Another is like it, namely, that the invitations ought to be towards the right. Sound the same? Yes it is, only this time I mean that the invitations ought to be towards the right, *not up or down the column*. Let me explain. It seems that people like to concentrate on one thing. If someone is asked to do too many things it doesn't allow them to concentrate on the one thing that is essential at that time. For example, if someone is going to a playgroup (= Pre-Evangelism), it doesn't make sense to ask them to a coffee morning with the same pre-evangelistic aim. It uses up their time a little more, and so competes with a more worthwhile activity that you may be able to invite them to. Let me say it again: no-one gets converted through pre-evangelism; they need to hear the gospel. No matter how many pre-evangelisms they are into, they still won't get converted. If they are in the playgroup then *no ground is made at all* if they are also invited to the coffee morning—in fact, ground may well be lost. What they need to be invited to is not something up or down the same column but something in the *next column to the right*. They need to be moved out of Pre-Evangelism into Evangelism.

There may come a time when they tire of one kind of pre-evangelism or outgrow it—for instance, their preschooler goes to school and they therefore cannot come to playgroup. Then, if such an activity is still thought necessary, it may be the time to invite her to the coffee morning. But it will be better still to get her out of pre-evangelism altogether and into something that will give her the gospel and help her to get converted. However, if pre-evangelism is all that she seems to want at this stage, then a (reluctant) invitation up or down the Pre-Evangelism column can be made. In doing so, however, we ought to realise that even though she may seem 'more involved' (because this will now be the second activity she has used), in terms of our mission goals, *absolutely no ground has been made*. Pre-evangelism remains pre-evangelism and nothing more. And, in case you have missed it so far I will say it again—it won't get anyone converted by itself.

Forward!

There is a third principle. Just as invitations should be towards the right, and invitations ought not to be up or down the same column at the same time, so also it is a firm rule that *you never move backwards*. This may be rule one in disguise, but it is important enough to say it anyway! (Let's call it a corollary of the rule about moving to the right.) If Mr Normal Brit—'Norm' for short—has just had a child and, for whatever reason felt only to him (and it *will* be felt, hardly ever *thought*), he approaches his local baby-baptizing institution, which happens to be your church, what do you do with him? Do you send him away so you can 'Raise his Awareness' first? No, he is not only aware of where the church is, but also that it provides a baptism service, and even that this is vaguely to do with 'God'. Do you try to establish Initial Contact with Norm, perhaps asking for his address so that the doorknock team can call on him to explain where your church is and that he would be welcome to come anytime? No! Don't be stupid. He's standing there on your doorstep: contact has been made —from his side, at least! Do you ask him along to a Pre-Evangelism activity so he can 'build relationships' with some of the people at church? No, you don't even need to do this. In fact, you *must not* do this—it is an invitation that moves him backwards. Norm hasn't arrived to 'build relationships'; he has arrived for the baptism of his child. In the present day situation, this usually means that he has kindly presented you with an opportunity for Evangelism. Now, if Norm is standing there asking to be evangelized, it is ridiculous to shove him into something that won't give him the gospel in a direct, forthright and clear way, asking him for a decision en route. Once Norm arrives on the doorstep there is only one kind of invitation he needs and that is the invitation of the gospel. You *never move backwards*.

What next?

Even if he doesn't respond to the first gospelling activity—in this case, the baptismal interviews in which it is your policy to share the gospel at least three times—and you want to know what to do next, you still don't move him backwards. Now is the time to bounce him up and down in the same column. He needs to be given as many opportunities to be evangelized as you've got going, one after the other, and then you have to invent some more! Never lose ground, always move ahead.

What if his interest seems to wane and nothing has happened? Well, some people may think a bit of Pre-Evangelism could be good for him —a couple of games of golf with the church men, an invitation to bring his family to the church barn dance or BBQ—and certainly this may be of some use. But (and here is what this principle is trying to drive home), once he has entered your scheme of things at the level of 'Please Evangelize Me', then you have to keep evangelizing him—that is the only polite thing to do! If he seems to cool off, perhaps the strategy should be to keep just the right amount of evangelistic pressure on him at the level he has reached so far. If he has done Christianity Explained and decided not to go on to your next evangelistic activity, you can still keep before him the challenge that Christianity Explained left him with: the occasional phone call, centring upon the decision that he knows he has to make; the occasional reminder to him about the urgency of deciding for Jesus. During this time, you may decrease the frequency with which you are inviting him to evangelistic *activities* but you should still maintain contact with him as *a person who needs, and now knows he needs, to make a decision for Christ*. And, of course, he knows that you will contact him when there is an important evangelistic activity on as well, for by now he knows that you want him to have as many opportunities as possible! But our point is clear: you *never move backwards*. Whatever your strategy with Norm, don't lose ground—always aim at evangelism.

As for the Christians of your congregation this aspect of the tool helps with them too, but this can wait until chapter 7.

You Watch Me, Me Watch You

There is one exception to these absolutely unbreakable rules! The one time when it is legitimate to give an invitation 'to the left' is when you wish to involve someone in an activity for the sake of their ministry. A keen Christian man may be invited to join an 'Investigating Christianity' group with five non-Christian men. Why? Not because he needs to be evangelized—for goodness sake, he is so thoroughly converted that the angels in heaven have long ago stopped their celebrations—but because you want him to learn how to evangelize others. He is in the group to watch you do it, so that he can then do it too, on his own eventually. (He will do a much better job after he watches you if you then watch him and give feedback for his further training. This is the YWMMWY method of training in ministry: You Watch Me, Me Watch You.). Someone may well get an invitation to the left, even though it is for another reason. It needs to be *for their sake*. And so it ends up being an invitation to the right, for it is an invitation to the column headed 'Training In Ministry'.

Watch this one. In Maintenance Mode these kind of invitations to 'Be Involved With X or Y' are often issued, mostly at the end of the year or at the beginning of a new one. They usually go like this: at announcement time in the church meeting someone stands up with a real worried look on his face and says, "There's a desperate need for more teachers in the Sunday School. You should all feel guilty if you don't meet this urgent need. The children of today are the church of tomorrow." He sits down and everyone *does* feel guilty. But no-one responds except for that young girl who can't say no to anything and is already running fourteen classes from the previous invitations! Notice how this kind of invitation works: we have a need in Structure X; therefore fill it up! People are dangled over a hole in a messy structure which needs patching.

This is not the way forward at all. Nobody ought to be doing a job—oops... that is not the way to say it. Nobody ought to have a ministry to a group of people unless they are gifted for that ministry and unless they themselves will benefit from being involved in it. Their sphere of service ought to be a help to their own Christian development—they should be getting trained as they serve. This doesn't mean that they aren't asked to do a thing until they decide they have the gifts or desire the training; that is not their privilege. It is their church's privilege and responsibility to open up ministries for them. But it does mean that the church ought to think long and hard about each person before inviting anyone to exercise a ministry anywhere.

Do you see the direction we are approaching things from? We don't move from the structure (with a gaping hole in it) to the people (who are now merely gap-fillers), but we move *from the people to the ministry* to which they are peculiarly suited in the opinion of their church. You see, if mission is about people and ministry is about people, then the converse is true as well: people are about ministry. But this is our next chapter. Let's leave it until then.

People mean ministry

Now that we are reoriented to think about ministry from the people end, the beauty of our tool becomes even more apparent. For it enables us to plan out a strategy for our ministry to each and every individual within our care.

Take out your (blue rectangular?) piece of paper and put the goals along the top once again. Above the left–hand column, write: 'Non-Christian contacts'. Then list out all the non-Christian people that you are seeking to bring to Christ—without whom they are lost; with whom they are gloriously saved. (This should be simply a re-listing of your prayer list—but I won't put it that way lest I make you feel guilty about lapsing into Maintenance Mode in your prayers as well.)

Now go across the columns and **analyse** what ministry each has received. How was their awareness raised? Do you know? If so, write it in. If not, why not ask them next time you visit them? How was initial contact made? Write it in. And was there a pre-evangelism bit to their story? Write it in. What opportunities to hear the gospel have you given them? List these out in the Evangelism column.

Having analysed your ministry to the first person on your list: what will be your next step? You learn fast, of course: **planning**. What evangelistic opportunity are you going to take with them next? Will you invite them to a short series of evangelistic Bible studies? Will you invite them to the guest service coming up next August? Will you go around and ask them the two 'Evangelism Explosion' questions (no doubt I should put a copyright symbol on these somewhere—make sure you do if you use them!)? Will you give them an evangelistic book or tape or video or...? Whatever it is, write in your plan, then grab your diary and arrange a time to do it.

	EVANGELISM			
Non–Christian Contacts	Raising Awareness	Initial Contact	Pre-Evangelism	Evangelism
Ima Nunbeliever	Newspaper advert	Phone call to me	–	Shared "2 Ways to Live" 6/2/89. Christianity Explained April–June 89 Guest service – July 89 Video given – August 89 <u>Plan</u>: – Invite to "Investigating Christianity" beginning Feb 90 – personal conversation: try to find out why he has not made a decision so far – ring and arrange <u>tonight</u>

It is now time to move onto the next person on your prayer list. What have you done? What will you do next? When will you do it?

Once you have gone through your non-Christian prayer list, have a breather, then get out your Christian prayer list or your church roll or your Bible Study group roll or your 'these are the people I have a ministry to' roll. Take out the now familiar blue rectangular piece of paper with the columns and put at the top of the left-hand side 'Church' (or something equally descriptive). Then put down number one: 'Alexander Aardvark'. What ministry have you exercised with his benefit in mind? Or what ministry is being exercised towards him and by whom (for it needn't and eventually cannot always be you)? Write it all down. Okay, now the planning: what (further) ministry does Big

Al need? Or, what (further) ministry does the one already having a ministry to Big Al need? Write it down, then get your diary and you know what comes next. Then do person number two. And so on.

The tool is also helpful in deciding what kind of ministry a person ought to be trained in. Grab another piece of blue, rectangular Mission Goals paper and give the left-hand column the heading 'Training in Ministry'. List out your key people (that is, anyone who is not an extremely new Christian, for every Christian will have a ministry of some kind—notice that even the blind man in John 9 and the cured Gerasene demoniac in Mark 5 weren't given too long to cool their heels before being sent off into the harvest field). Now begin to think about training them in ministry. How will you do it?

Whatever you do must be helpful to them and a fitting avenue for their gifts to be used. Use the tool to think about them.

- *Raising Awareness*: Is Mr Aardvark someone who could write the copy for a weekly newspaper advertisement? Is he retired with plenty of energy, enough for a daily walk during which he could drop leaflets in letterboxes? Has the doctor ordered him a daily walk following his triple by-pass—an even stronger indication of his spiritual giftedness in this area?!
- *Initial Contact:* Is he a friendly, outgoing sort of guy who has the ability to make people feel relaxed and comfortable? Would he be suitable for the doorknock team, or the 'Welcomers' at church on Sunday morning?
- *Evangelism:* Does he know the gospel? Is he keen to save the lost? Can he explain the gospel? Has he been already doing this?
- *Edification:* Does he know his Bible well? Is he an able teacher? Is he reliable?

And so on. Then turn to your diary and arrange a time at which you can get together with AA, talk over his giftedness and thrust him into the ministry he is suited for. At the same time you can outline the training opportunities that he will be given and how he will receive the ongoing encouragement that every Christian should receive as they are involved in ministry. Now for the next person on your list.

Once all this hard work is over, it becomes obvious that such thinking enables you to care more effectively for the most valuable resource your church has got: its people. Once a person's Training in Ministry opportunity is decided (with their consultation and agreement, of course), then it will prevent everyone from being over-committed, mobilize more people into ministry, prevent burn out, and even stop the gap-filling approach, because all the gaps will be filled before they even open up!

I know what you are saying: "Where am I going to get the time to do all this? It is far easier to just keep the group going as it is." That is true. Maintenance is easier than mission. But it is also far less effective. Paul wrote: "We proclaim him, admonishing and teaching everyone with all wisdom, so that we may present everyone perfect in Christ. To this end I labour, struggling with all his energy, which so powerfully works in me" (Col 1:28-29). His ministry was directed towards 'everyone', that is, each person at an individual, personal level. It involved all the God-given energy that he had. And he used it because the goal of maturity/perfection for all was so important in the plan of God. Surely this should be our pattern of ministry as well. Isn't ministry about encouraging each person onwards towards maturity in Christ? If we feel we have too little time to plan out a ministry strategy for each individual, perhaps that indicates it is time to share the load. Is this why Paul had his team around him—Timothy and the rest? Is it time to more actively involve other elders in the church in such caring for people? Is it time we put on another pastor? Enlisted more helpers for the ministry? Prayed for more labourers to be sent out into the harvest field?

Mission means people. People mean ministry. Our tool can help us focus upon our mission (which is Christ's mission), and provide ministry to our people (who are Christ's people). And it is not just helpful to a pastor of a church—anyone involved in ministry to any group of people can get out that blue sheet of paper and work out a strategy for their ministry to the members of their youth group or Bible Study or the people at work or school or whatever. Mission means people; people mean ministry.

But one more thing remains. Ministry needs to be supported in various ways, and the tool can help here as well. It is to this new and different category of 'Support to Ministry' that we now turn.

Supporting Christian ministry

I know I'm doing something naughty by making a distinction between 'Ministry' (i.e. something that directly serves the gospelling or edification of people) and 'Support to Ministry'. However, I feel that it is a useful distinction, for it enables us to keep the focus on our mission goals and see how other things serve these goals. It is all too easy for things in this supportive category to gain an importance that they don't warrant. Take, for instance, a working bee. Sure, it does *indirectly* serve the work of the kingdom, but it only does so *indirectly*. If we hold a working bee every day of the week until Christ returns, nobody will be converted, and nobody will necessarily progress towards maturity. It does not contribute *directly* to the work of ministry, although no doubt it would contribute directly to the work of blisters. Or take committee work and its office bearers, who are often given the status that goes with personalized nametags printed with their title underneath in oversized capitals. Sure, they do a job that is necessary and important, and, biblically speaking, it is a ministry—probably the gift of 'helps and administrations' (1 Cor 12:28). But if all the Christian church did was run committee meetings, the kingdom of God would not advance very far. And unfortunately there is a lot of evidence in many churches and across denominations to back up that claim! To separate 'Support to Ministry' into its own category enables such roles and meetings to function with a clear idea of what they are doing: *they are never an end in themselves, but they support the real work of the gospel.*

The same goes for the various rosters; morning tea, washing up, gardening, cleaning, etc. These are all supportive ministries in that they support the ministry of the gospel. It is all too easy for people to be on every cleaning roster and at every working bee and be elected to wear every nametag that's going, and then have no time or inclination or feel any compulsion to be involved in the real work. If we let people see that such things are ministries in the same category as Evangelism and Edification, then the excuse 'I did my bit for the church—the working bee takes three hours of my time each month' becomes perfectly valid. In this busy world that is a lot of time! Every year, most churches have an Annual General Meeting which forces us to elect office bearers to Support the Ministry. The danger is that this annual pressure might put good people into supportive roles, when they should be in ministry roles. Time often says that they can't do both, and so we may have the ludicrous situation in which the talents of people who should be leading Bible studies or preaching the gospel or training others in ministry have been hijacked, leaving them to fall asleep at the monthly committee meeting. The mission goals should help us to maintain priorities: encourage those gifted people to get into ministry, and let others take care of supporting the ministry. The danger is that so many people can be used up *supporting* the ministry that no-one is *doing* the (much harder but far more rewarding) ministry that will actually win the lost and edify and equip the saints.

There are other things that can be called a Support to Ministry—the weekly prayer meeting, for example. So often, prayer meetings can degenerate into asking God to heal Aunt Mildred's sore toenail. (What, is that *still* a problem? It must be—no matter where you pray or when you pray it seems to always come up!) Now, of course God likes dealing with ingrown toenails as much as the rest of us, and it ought to be prayed for by someone, somewhere. But at the church prayer meeting? Every week? By so many people? By making it known that the prayer meeting is a Support to Ministry, the prayers are immediately focused on the mission **goals** that this church is working towards, on the **people** targeted to be reached, on the **edification** of the congregation, on **those being trained** for ministry. Now *there* is a prayer meeting! And because the goals are drawn from the Bible, we know that we are praying according to God's will. And let me tell you, that prayer meeting will be an exciting thing to be a part of as God does what he promises and answers prayers time and again!

The "M" Word

Then there is giving. Yes, I am talking about money. Why do we pass the plate around at everything bar the morning tea (you *do*!)? Isn't it to support the mission of this church? Isn't it to provide resources that are needed to further the goals that we have? Isn't it to support the ministry of the gospel? This focuses our giving, for without this financial support perhaps the goals will not be reached as effectively. Giving can't be an end in itself. The person who does his bit for the church by tossing his twenty cents in the plate may be supporting the ministry (fairly minimally, no doubt), but he is still not being trained in the ministry or being part of it yet. (What goal do you have for him on your blue piece of paper?) He is merely *supporting* the ministry, not *doing* it.

Having justified the distinction a little, I also need to add that this tool can help us with these Supports to Ministry. We have already seen how the Mission goals can focus a prayer meeting, and how they can help a pastor or committee analyse and plan. But committees have other functions as well. After planning according to the Mission goals, they can then review and monitor progress throughout the year, and keep things going according to the goals they set for the various activities. They usually have some role in funding various activities, and the goals can shape the apportioning of funds. The treasurer can get out his blue (usually pin-striped) piece of paper, put 'Money' at the top of the left-hand column and list out all the things that money is spent on in the budget. He can then go across the goals columns and fill in his dark boxes to see what goals are being funded by this church. Is the cash going into Ministry or is it going into Support for Ministry (buildings, grounds, etc.)? It is a good idea for budgets to be set after the planning of goals, so that the committee first asks *What should we do?* and only then asks *How shall we fund our goals?, not How much have we got?* then *What will we spend it on?*

When looking at our strategy for our ministry to people (our most valuable resource), this perhaps unbiblical distinction does come in handy. Are a lot of man-hours and cash and resources being spent on activities that are, in the end, only Support to Ministry? The danger is that if too many resources are being drained by Support to Ministry then there may not end up being any Ministry to support!

A related issue which can now be discussed (since we have now discussed the entire piece of paper) is the question of what and how much people ought to be involved in. It is easy to find people that are overburdened in the work of their church and, sadly, there are some whose overwork for the church helps them to forget the one they are meant to be serving. There are even people who burn out from too much church work, and end up burning out from Christian discipleship altogether. It is just as easy to think of people who don't contribute anything much to Christ's mission, but who have the view that they take what they please and have no obligation to give anything back.

We have already seen that the tool can aid our ministry to people. (In itself, the tool is therefore a support to ministry!) As we think about the people in our congregation we can put their names in the left-hand column and then map out the things they are involved in.

	EVANGELISM				EDIFICATION			SUPPORT TO MINISTRY
People	Raising Awareness	Initial Contact	Pre-Evangelism	Evangelism	Follow-up	Nurture	Training in Ministry	
John Smith	•Writes newspaper ad weekly	•Door-knock team	• Runs Men's mechanics night	•Monthly dialogue meeting •Hosts Christianity Explained	–	•Sunday church (2 services) • Thurs Bible study • Tues Bible study • Correspondence course	• Leads Sunday School class • Runs Yth group	• Working bee • Committee (Secretary) • Giving • Prayer meeting
Sally Green	–	–	–	–	–	• Sunday Church (fortnightly)	–	–

Then it gets difficult. It seems obvious that John Smith is doing far too much (how does he fit in his job as corporate executive of one of the largest companies in the country, and his wife and seven children, and his sick parents who live with them, and...) and Sally Green has a fairly minimal involvement. But, what is the 'normal requirement' for a Christian engaged in Christ's Mission? What can be normally expected from each member of your congregation? It is a fact of life that people cannot be involved in all things going and expect to do all things well. It is also a fact of life that different people have different capacities and circumstances. But there may be some rule of thumb that can be worked out.

For a start, a person should be at the weekly congregational meeting (usually known as the 'Church Service') in which the Word of God is publicly proclaimed and prayers are said in response. This is a time when the Word of God sets the agenda for the work of the gospel in the week to come, a 'rallying point' for this group of Christians. Secondly, it is fairly usual nowadays to have a small group network in which the Word of God is discussed and applied and prayers are said in a more personal way than is possible in the weekly public meeting. The third expectation might be that every person is engaged in one thing for the purpose of ministry, since we should also be giving of ourselves to others, and whatever gifts we have been given are for the good of other people. Then, at the end of the list, there may also be a Support to Ministry activity that some people can also be involved in.

Once such 'Normal Expectations' are decided upon, at least as a rule of thumb, this enables you to talk with people about their 'load' and to suggest that they correct any deficiencies or drop any extra burdens that are spreading them too thin. In this process, of course, they will be moving into areas for which they are most gifted and out of those that others are more suited to.

Back to the program

Back in Chapter 3, we talked about the structures that you might already find in place. Since then we have covered quite a lot of country, discovering en route, amongst other things, that ministry is 'people not programs'. That may be a great relief to you. Every time it comes time to plan your program for the year or the month or even the day, you may go into a catatonic spasm for all I know, and so hearing this slogan is like hearing the good news of the gospel all over again! "No more programs!" I hear you yelling in delight, "No more planning! No more juggling dates! No more lining up events and speakers and ... No more ...."

Well, I'm sorry to break in upon this time of glee, but I have to. For the slogan 'People not Programs' is meant to focus our priorities; it is not meant to imply that there should be no programs at all. We do need a program, but it needs to have its proper place. It needs to serve the people. It needs to help them in their mission-oriented ministry.

Unfortunately, programs don't just happen—they need planning. The first step towards planning a program is to **plan when you will plan it**. At one end of the scale you have a daily routine, and at the other you have a yearly program. In between you have a weekly routine, and you may operate by month, or by school term. Whatever units of time you operate with, it is a good idea to set some time aside to plan your program for that time unit. And, of course, if you take the trouble to plan, it is also necessary to keep reviewing whether and how much you have achieved your plans, and so a regular time for **review** is also necessary.

But what enables such planning to be effective? Of course you know by now! The planning at the daily or weekly or monthly or term level will only be effective if the 'big picture' has also been worked out. That is, the logical order is to decide what our mission goals are—and our tool has provided that already—and then to plan an integrated overall program for the people in our church that aims to be as helpful to their mission as it can possibly be. This 'big picture' should generate the yearly program, and the yearly the monthly, and the monthly the weekly, and the weekly the daily. This means that, once the mission goals are adopted, a good period of time needs to be given to planning the year to come (and no doubt also reviewing the year that has just passed). Given the patterns in most churches, April/May seems to be a good time to do this. As for time needed, since it is so important, why not set aside a whole week to do it, perhaps planning to hold meetings with key groups and individuals to aid in this task?

But how do you plan an *integrated* and *mission helping* program? To do so, there seem to be three aspects of a church program that require thought. There are the regular 'maintenance' type structures, which, as we now understand, maintain people in their task of mission. There is the yearly program of events and activities, which, as we now understand, ought to help people in their task of mission. And there is the personal program of the pastor, which, as we will soon understand, ought to equip, facilitate and enthuse people for their task of mission.

1. Proper Maintenance

In Ephesians 4:15, Paul informs us that Christ's body (i.e. the congregation) grows as we speak the truth in love. Here he furnishes us with the key to proper maintenance: truth being spoken in love. This takes place at three levels: publicly, privately and individually.

Publicly
The truth ought to be spoken publicly at the regular congregational meetings/church services. Regular and systematic biblical preaching

is essential to maintain the mission focus for a church. And, dare I say it, the preaching should be expository (that is, gradually seeking to explain the text of the Scriptures) rather than topical (that is, seeing what the Bible says on a topic of interest to us). Can you see why? If we are interested in being involved in *God's* mission, we need to allow him to set the agenda for us by dealing with the Bible in the way that he revealed it, rather than subtly setting our own agenda by always addressing the Bible with *our* questions and issues. Expository preaching allows the Word to address the world, and results in us seeing that world with God's eyes. Topical preaching allows the world to address the Word and results in us seeing both the world and the Word with our own eyes.

Having said that, there *is* a place for the topic—it can be used as exactly that: a topic. Once a preacher has understood the passage he will expound, he needs to ask himself: "How does this portion of God's Word address our world? What questions, desires, hopes, dreams, problems and pains does it address?" He can then use his answer to mould an appropriate topic for his expositional sermon. Remember my point: the members of the congregation need to be constantly reminded of the mission in which they are involved, and the goals which they are meant to pursue, and it is God's Word that will do this as it is regularly expounded in a systematic way. For then it is the Word which sets the agenda for both preacher and people.

Since the sermon is God's Word being addressed to a particular gathering of people, it ought to be the centre of whatever else occurs on Sunday (or whenever your church meets). Because God is at work in our midst, we should expect and plan for the fact that people will be present from all kinds of backgrounds—they may be converted or they may be still ignorant of God when they walk through the door that morning. Because the Word of God is addressed to any person present in the meeting, the whole meeting should be tailored so that no-one is hindered from hearing the Word of God. The Word of God for the day should issue in realistic prayer for the world and the congregation and their mission in the world. The songs should be selected as appropriate expressions of the joy that comes from hearing the Word of God yet again. In fact, the tone of everything that goes on should be filled with both the seriousness of listening to the living God, and the marvelous and deep joy that comes from hearing what he says. And then there is the love that needs to be present, not just love for those in the club, those so like ourselves, but the love of Christ for a lost world—the lost world that is there in our midst right at that very moment! The tragedy is that sometimes the things we do in church seem to ignore the fact that there is a world 'out there'.

Why say all this now? This vital part of the program also needs to be *planned*: what parts of the Bible will the preaching program include this year? What truth will be proclaimed publicly as part of the proper maintenance the congregation needs?

Privately

Then there is the proper maintenance that goes on privately. The basic unit, biblically speaking, is the family. In that setting, the truth of God ought to be spoken in love in the middle of all the ordinary pursuits of life (see Deut 6:4-9, Eph 6:4, 1 Cor 14:35). Certainly a church can plan ways to encourage and assist this kind of private teaching, and therefore make it part of the congregation's program. But it cannot be planned for in the same way as another private means of speaking the truth in love, that is, the small group network that exists within so many churches today.

Small groups perform functions that the public meeting cannot hope to do as adequately. They enable people to interract over God's Word, to ask questions, hear answers, to share applications, to pray together for more personal concerns, to learn to love whomever has been thrown together by the group, to begin to exercise gifts, to pray by name for the conversion of each other's non-Christian friends, to share the joy of seeing prayers answered, to receive personal attention and pastoral care from a small group of people and especially from the group leader, who really performs the role of pastor to that group. The fact is that when God causes a church to grow, it is this network of small groups that provides the context in which much of the pastoral care of a congregation goes on. One person cannot hope to care adequately for an entire congregation. With an adequate small group ministry, there is no need for one person to try!

An important step in planning, then, is to think about this very significant network where the Word of God is spoken in love privately. Are there adequate small groups to care for all the people in the congregation? If there are *in*adequate groups, then it will be hard to encourage everyone to join a group. The experts say that a good group number is about 8-12 people, so you can easily do the sums: in a congregation of 60 you need 5-7 groups; a congregation of 120 will need 10-15. Are there enough groups now? Will there be enough for the end of the year, after God 'adds to your numbers daily'? If not, your planning must include their increase.

And of course, that entails an increase in group leaders. This is often where the plot fails, for after all there is only one person in your entire congregation with nine and a half years of theological training, and you're already too busy! But don't be put off. Remember, firstly, that God causes gifts to emerge to meet needs—so pray! Then, secondly, remember that there are a variety of ways a group can be lead—a leader can do it all from his vast storehouse of wisdom and knowledge, or everyone can have a go with suitable direction from someone ready and able, or prepared material can be used, tapes can be listened to and discussed, videos can be be watched, or a combination of many different things. And the good thing is that whoever leads or co-ordinates will be far better at it by the end of the year than they are now! So plan who your new leaders will be—if not this year, than certainly by next year, and then plan how you will use this year to get them ready. How will you train your new (and existing) leaders for their ministry. Plan a monthly leaders meeting. Plan the input you will give, and so on.

Then, of course, you need to plan how you are going to encourage people to join these groups. Public announcements? Public testimonies to their value? (When, how, how often?) Personal visits to encourage people to join particular groups? And so on.

Individually
The final place for speaking the truth in love is individually, one to one. Hopefully this will be a by-product of the public and private teaching of God's Word. But that is not all that can be done. Each member of the congregation needs to be stretched further in their understanding and practice of the Word of God and there are ways to help them in this. Do you want to plan a Bible reading promotion? Do you want to have a session with your Bible Study Group leaders to 'gee them up', so that they can gee their group members up? Is there a good biblical correspondence course that key people can do? Do you want to embark on a personal visit of everyone on your roll to talk over the Bible input habits they may or may not have? And how can you help people to share their insights from God's Word with each other? Do you want to plan a 'sharing time' in the public meeting, or as a regular feature of the home group program? What about a system for pairing or 'tripletting' up the congregation so that people have someone specific to talk with about what they have been learning? And on it goes.

Such public, private, and individual "speaking the truth in love" needs to be planned into the life of a church, for it provides the substructure, the strong foundation, the proper kind of maintenance for a church seeking to be 'mission minded'.

2. The Yearly Program

With the substructure of proper maintenance planned for, our attention can turn to the yearly program. What events and activities will help the congregation's mission this year?

Since people tend to be future-oriented, it is a good idea to schedule several key events that can focus the yearly program. Since we are now in mission mode, armed with our trusty piece of blue, en-columned paper, it is fairly obvious that these key events ought to reflect our priorities. In other words, make the key events gospel events. For example, why not schedule two periods of increased evangelistic activity (I have to say 'increased' because we are now in mission mode and so evangelism ought to be on the agenda at all times)? For two consecutive weeks in both April and August you might plan to hold a guest service to which people can bring their friends, and in which there will be an opportunity for people to become Christians.

Now, how can these events provide the integration for your program? Well, for the month prior to these events your congregation will need to be inviting their friends to come, and so invitation cards/ leaflets will need to be ready by then. As well as this, all of the people who attend the activities listed in your Pre-Evangelism column will be offended if they are not asked, so their 'inviters' need to be mobilised to do a lot of visits and phone calls during this month. Then there are the names on your own non-Christian contact list—be prepared for a large phone bill that month!

Since the last such event was held around the time that Noah put away his raincoat, you figure that the congregation may be a little rusty/ fearful/inept at inviting people. Solution? You will hold a training session or two to walk people through their fears, the process of invitation, the importance of doing it, and to pray with them about this 'Invitation Month'.

In fact, why not get them praying as early as possible? Attendance at the monthly prayer meeting could be encouraged, since there are now some specific agenda items to pray for. The home groups could pray as a group for new contacts to invite in various places around them—that new housing district that is still not represented in church; the high school over the road; that ethnic group that is so over-represented at the shopping centre, but so under-represented in your church; their work places; that private drinking club around the corner; the local sports club; etc. Prayer cards could be issued upon which friends names could be written; pairs or triplets could regularly meet to pray through these names. You also know that there are a few people who will really take to the idea of these increased evangelism seasons, since they are already keen to share their faith with others. But you also know that they have real struggles with how to do it. With evangelism in the wind, why not invite them to do a 'How to share your faith in four easy lessons' course with you in September? They can then be given the ministry of chatting with any people who respond during the November meetings (you must expect that some will respond—God is at work, isn't he?). Some of them can then be given the opportunity to inflict the 'How to share your faith in four easy lessons' course on others before the March Increased Evangelism Season.

And don't forget to plan what will happen after these events as well. When people respond, who will be the first to contact them? They will need to have a clear diary the week immediately after the meetings. Then who will do the initial follow-up? When will these people be trained? Will you have a nurture/newcomers group? Who will lead it and how will they be trained?

September	October
• Form prayer triplets • Evangelism Training Course #1 • Invitation Training Seminar #1	• Invitation month • Two special prayer meetings
November • Two guest services, then • Initial visit week • Follow up/nurture group begins	**December** • Follow up/nurture group continues
January • Form more prayer triplets • Evangelism Training Course #2	**February** • Invitation month • Two special prayer meetings
March • Two guest services, then • Initial visit week • Follow up/nurture group begins	**April** • Follow up/nurture group continues

As you can see, it doesn't take very long before your yearly program is quite full, and the beauty is that, if you allow your evangelistic events to focus the program, it is full of activities that are thoroughly mission-oriented. Once the planning is done, you could take it around to all the leaders of your groups, as well as a blank copy of your new-found handy little assessment tool, and discuss with them the function of their group and where it might fit into the church's overall vision. People love to know where they fit into the 'big picture', and this discussion will be most fruitful indeed. Then the home groups, other groups, families and individuals can also focus their prayers and activities around this program.

Planning your program also enables your public meetings to be focussed, for it provides some specifics to pray for and advertise. Can I pause on this point briefly? It seems that the advertising slot in churches is the one fixed point in their 'liturgy'; even churches that claim no liturgy will be completely liturgical about 'The Notices'. The equally ubiquitous 'Pew Bulletin' usually provides the script for the person giving 'The Notices'. It seems to me that this advertising time is often completely useless, because its importance is easily overlooked. Just setting the congregation's mission goals using your bit of paper will not mean that they will think in a mission-centred manner. The 'vision' of these biblical goals will constantly need to be put before them, so that they begin to think, breathe, walk, talk, sleep and eat these goals! Once these mission goals are enshrined in the congregation's yearly program, one way to keep the vision alive is to *advertise well*.

And what do you advertise? Often the liturgical 'Notices' spot is open for anyone who thrusts a note in the hand of the minister before the service. Those days are over. The advertisements in the public meeting should reflect the vision of the congregation as a whole. So what do you advertise? You advertise the key events on your program, and you do it in an enthusiastic, positive, 'let's-all-get-amongst-it' kind of way. This strategy of advertising only the events on the congregational program will require some thought about how you will cope with things that people will invariably want to advertise. You might, for example, take a 'multi-media' approach, in which certain items (e.g. regular events, church committee, home group leaders meetings) appear in the 'bulletin' and people are trained to read this sheet for things that they are involved with. Other material that may be of interest to only some and slightly peripheral to your congregation's concerns could be put on a notice board near the morning tea area for people to browse through (e.g. the local FE College wants help teaching English to migrants; there is a jobsearch seminar on; a Christian band is playing for the youth group in the neighbouring church). Then there will be other material that is of no help to your congregation, and perhaps even harmful—and why shouldn't that go straight in the round file?

What have we covered under this point? The program of events needs to be planned and it can be integrated using specifically evangelistic events. Such an integrated program can constantly focus the activities of a congregation, and, as the various groups incorporate themselves into the 'big picture', and as it is advertised well, it can keep the congregational vision in everyone's view.

3. The Pastor's Personal Program

Anyone who has a group of people under their care is a pastor to some degree, so these things are relevant to any group leader, sunday school teacher, etc who has to plan a program, even if I seem to be addressing *the* pastor much of the time. The difference between these kinds of pastors and *the* pastor is one of scope. It is the usual practice—and with good biblical precedent I might add—that congregations have some kind of pastor (or pastoral team) that oversees, not just a portion of the congregation, but the congregation as a whole. This role is extremely important, for the overall pastor must provide good biblical leadership for the congregation, both through his explicit teaching and through his own life. This mission–minded tool may help a pastor plan his own program as well.

It can help him care for the congregation's valuable people resource, as touched on earlier. Is each person receiving pastoral care from somebody? If they are a newcomer, who in the congregation is in touch with them? If they are an inquirer, who is answering their questions? If they are newly converted, who is following them up? If they are Christians beyond that initial stage, which Bible Study Group are they in? How are they being developed and stretched? What gifts do they have, and how can they be further trained to fulfill their ministry? In terms of their life and ministry, where do we want them to be in 12 months time? How can our congregation help to get them there?

We have also seen that it can help the pastor to plan the overall program, to understand the function of all the groups and activities, and to discuss this function with the group/activity leaders.

But it can also help organize his own personal program. Take Pastor Tom. He's been flat out for many years now in a church that has been around for many more years. And, yes, in the quietness of a dark corner somewhere, but only in the presence of (one or maybe two) friends, Tom may even admit to feeling discouraged from time to time because he feels that maybe he is in perpetual Maintenance mode. He wants to think Mission. He finds your scrappy bit of blue paper after you left it on the bus, and he decides to analyse *himself*.

What should he be doing? As a preacher of the gospel, and (if it is a different thing) a teacher of the Scriptures, he is someone set aside from working for a living, to devote himself to the ministry of the Word of God and to prayer. This ministry ought to be shaped by mission goals as well, shouldn't it? At the top of the left hand column he writes 'My ministry', and proceeds to list all the things that he finds himself engaged in during a normal month of ministry. Then he takes a big breath and takes a long look at the result:

People	EVANGELISM				EDIFICATION			SUPPORT to MINISTRY
	Raising Awareness	Initial Contact	Pre-Evangelism	Evangelism	Follow-up	Nurture	Training in Ministry	
Sunday Service + preaching						�		
Scripture Teaching	▢	▯	▢	▯				
Committees (x4)								▢
Organize rosters								▢
Bible Study (x1)						▢		
Baptism inquiries (phone)		▢						
Marriages		▢▢						
Funerals		▢						
Hospital visits (congregation + non)						▢		
Men's night		▢						

He decides that his new mission-centred mind doesn't like everything he sees on the paper. He grabs a fresh piece, and writes the heading 'My ideal ministry' and proceeds to list the things he would like to be involved in, now that his ministry is mission.

What should he do? Well, he remembers that he is first and foremost a gospel preacher—at least in theory. That is what he has been trained for, and that is what his church has commissioned him for. He is the one who doesn't have to support himself, in order that he can be free to devote himself to prayer and the ministry of the Word of God. So he had better do that with all his energy! He has always put a high status on his preaching, and prepares his sermons very well. But have they been mission focussed? Come to think of it, there have been more than enough topical sermons—he finds it easier to say what's on his heart, than to do the hard work of preparing an unfamiliar passage from Zechariah! He decides to commit himself to expository sermons, so that his preaching ministry will be shaped by God's agenda, not his. And then there is the focus of his sermons. He admits to himself that he very rarely directs his sermons to people as people; he tends to always talk as if everyone in church is a Christian, and fairly keen about it. Perhaps he needs to have more awareness of the variety of people listening to him, and cast a wider net in his preaching. Maybe he should try to preach what God's word says to anyone and everyone who lives in this messed-up world. That would make it much easier for his congregation to bring anyone they know along to church whenever the opportunity presented itself, and they would be guaranteed of hearing something relevant.

	EVANGELISM				EDIFICATION			SUPPORT to MINISTRY
	Raising Awareness	Initial Contact	Pre-Evangelism	Evangelism	Follow-up	Nurture	Training in Ministry	
Expository preaching, focused widely								

What else should he do? He looks at the Evangelism column, and it is a sorry sight indeed. He's never really felt all that gifted in the area—he is more of a teacher than an evangelist. But, he thinks, Paul could say "imitate me as I imitate Christ", and he was talking about taking the

63

gospel to people to get them saved (1 Cor 11:1). And he could tell Timothy —poor old timid Timothy—to "do the work of an evange-list", which probably indicates that he didn't see himself as an evangelist but had to do the work anyway (2 Tim 4:5)! And besides, if the pastor is never seen evangelizing, how will the congregation follow his model? Well, they will—they won't evangelize either.

Our very self-analytic Tom continues to think, deep down: *I don't want to evangelize, because it fills me with fear.* But then, isn't everyone fearful? Even Paul sometimes felt the pressure and "despaired even of life" (2 Cor 1:8), and he had to ask for prayer that he would be more bold (Eph 6:19-20). It seems that he presented a model not of someone who had it all together as an evangelist, but of someone who was just as likely to go to jelly as the next man! But that was his point, for he was an example of someone whose weakness was his strength, because in his weakness it was very clear that any 'success' was God's work, not his (2 Cor 1:8-11; 11:16-12:11, and 1 Cor 2:1-5).

Tom suddenly realises that in all his fearful reluctance to evangelize he suddenly becomes the perfect model of an evangelist. He can model how to keep taking the opportunities God provides *despite his fear*; how to fail *and get up again for more;* how to have a priceless treasure in an old cracked cup (2 Cor 4:7-12); how to be just and always a beggar, but one who can point others to where they can find bread. Tom suddenly realises that the only criterion for doing the work of an evangelist is not ability or temperament or strength of desire to do it—the only criterion is that we have believed a message about God's overwhelming grace that wants to spread to more and more people (2 Cor 4:13-15). "I believed; therefore I have spoken," says Paul. And Tom resolves to say the same thing from now on, with God's help. His mind is racing: "My evangelistic edge needs to be constantly modelled in *public* (Do my sermons say something to the insider and the outsider?), in *private* (Do our prayer meetings and home group pray for people's conversion? Why doesn't my home group have the occasional dialogue meeting where non-Christian friends can come to hear the gospel and have their questions answered?), and with *individuals* (I could ask people how and when they were converted? I could seriously try to turn conversations to the gospel more often? I should expect people to become Christians, show them how, invite them to do so and offer to pray with them on the spot)". It seems that from now on, our Tom is planning to model evangelism.

What else should he do? Ephesians 4:11-12 and 2 Timothy 2:2 come to his mind, and it dawns on him that he has a unique responsibility and opportunity to train his congregation for their various ministries in the body of Christ. He should be training people. That column needs to be chock-a-block for this pastor! As he prays for people he should be asking for the wisdom to discern their gifts and the opportunity to push them ahead in their Christian life and ministry. He can think of a ready made opportunity for training straight away. Although he hasn't been taking advantage of them as much as he should, he suddenly realises that he probably has many more opportunities to take the gospel to people than anyone he knows, simply by virtue of being the pastor. Why doesn't he plan to always take people with him when he visits or teaches scripture or preaches as a guest somewhere else, so that they can watch him share the gospel? Then, after they have watched, they can try themselves, and he can watch them and give them feedback. Then, when they are ready for it, they could take someone else with them into their gospel opportunities and train them, and he could train them how to train them. If enough people were doing it, perhaps they could arrange to go on evangelistic visits for one particular night each week. They could all meet for prayer and a bit of input, and then go off to share the gospel on their visits. Then there are other training opportunities, such as running courses, all the regular meetings, special leaders meetings and so on. This has really got him thinking! He finishes writing out his 'Ideal Tom' sheet. (See over page.)

Of course, life is never ideal, and there are a few things he sees on the list that he would rather not see on it (labelled with an asterisk), but until he can get rid of them elsewhere, he'll keep them on for the time being. But simply by doing this exercise, he has now been made aware of an area that he will 'peel off' as soon as someone else comes along who is more eminently suited to that area than he is

And, of course, the next thing he will need to do is to plan his own personal program. Each week his schedule needs to reflect his priorities. He needs to fill in the blanks according to his mission goals, rather than waiting for others to fill in the blanks for him. And, once again, he needs to have some flexibility, for things do 'come up' that may be worthwhile in the long run (after all, God is ultimately in charge of our time, not us)—so why not plan some 'slush time' that can be filled if and when it is needed. The asterisked items may also find a place on the weekly timetable, but their fate is hanging in the balance now that their true worth has been evaluated!

A lot more could no doubt be said, but we have to stop talking somewhere. This tool needs to prove its usefulness as we begin to use it in our real-life setting.

Ideal Tom	EVANGELISM				EDIFICATION			SUPPORT to MINISTRY
	Raising Awareness	Initial Contact	Pre-Evangelism	Evangelism	Follow-up	Nurture	Training in Ministry	
Preaching			☐ ▓	▓	▓	▓	☐	
Bible Study				☐		▓	▓	
Newcomer's B/S				☐	▓			
B/S leaders training							▓	
Visits – baptism				▓			▓	
– marriage			☐ ▓				▓	
– funerals		☐		▓			▓	
– hospital		☐		▓			▓	
– SS parents				▓			▓	
–YG "				▓			▓	
– non-Xn husbands of church wives				▓			▓	
– congrega-tion				▓	▓	▓		
Training night							▓	
Men's night			▓ ☐					
★ Scripture	▓ ☐		☐	▓			▓	
★ Organize rosters								▓
★ Commit-tees								▓

One last comment remains, and then it is over to you.

Over to you!

9

So now you have it. A tool that is simple but extremely versatile. It enables anyone to become mission minded—to centre their ministry on mission. Perhaps some more specific objectives need to be filled in alongside these general, biblical goals, but nevertheless the mission goals discussed here will go a long way towards keeping the Mafia from your door! But, far more importantly, these goals will go a long way towards helping establish a mission-centred ministry, and this will help to bring the gospel to a lost world. If they manage to get us out of a maintenance rut, and so help others find their way into heaven, then it is worth the hard work of thinking, analysing, planning and implementing them, isn't it? What a great thought that is!

We have many good intentions, yet often they aren't enough to enable the exercise of a planned, purposeful and strategic ministry. Perhaps this simple tool on a now crumpled piece of blue rectangular paper will help us get involved and stay involved in Christ's all-important mission to seek and to save the lost. I pray that it does at least that, even if your bit of paper isn't blue. But now, it's over to you.

To make it easier, we've given you a photocopy master over the page. Blow it up to A3 on the colour of your choice...

	EVANGELISM				EDIFICATION			SUPPORT TO MINISTRY
	Raising Awareness	Initial Contact	Pre-Evangelism	Evangelism	Follow-up	Nurture	Training in Ministry	

St Matthias Press

Tools to get the job done

At St Matthias Press our aim is to produce a range of quality, evangelical materials which help Christians get the job of Gospel-oriented ministry done effectively. Whether it's in evangelism, follow-up, nurture or training in ministry (those now very familiar categories!) St Matthias Press has materials to help you. Here's a sample of some of our tools:

The Interactive Bible Study series...

BEYOND EDEN (GENESIS 1-11)

The first eleven chapters of the Bible are full of cataclysmic events—the creation of the world, the fall of mankind, the flood. But what is their significance for 20th (soon to be 21st) Century Christians? Looking back at Genesis from this side of Christ, what are we to make of it? *Beyond Eden* leads you on a voyage of discovery to find life-changing answers to these questions. Authors: Phillip Jensen and Tony Payne. £3.50

THE GOOD LIVING GUIDE (MATTHEW 5:1-12)

The Beatitudes are among the best-known verses in the Bible, but have you ever taken the time to find out what they really mean? *The Good Living Guide* unlocks the treasures of the Beatitudes by going back to the Old Testament. It will not only help you discover afresh the meaning of Matthew 5:1-12, but will teach you how to understand the New Testament by learning the message of the Old. And most importantly of all, you will have the painful but exhilarating experience of being challenged by the words of Jesus. Authors: Phillip Jensen and Tony Payne. £2,95

THE COMPLETE CHRISTIAN (COLOSSIANS)

What is the normal Christian life? What should Christians expect to experience? Is it simply a case of 'trust and obey' or is that too simplistic? The Apostle Paul's short letter to the Colossians offers simple but marvellous answers to these questions. For new Christians who want to be sure that they're on the right track, or for longer-serving Christians who are bedazzled by the range of alternatives on offer, *The Complete Christian* sheds bright light from God's Word. Authors: Phillip Jensen and Tony Payne. £2.95

THE PATH TO GODLINESS (TITUS)

Down the centuries, Christians have suffered from the effects of two damaging (and opposite) problems. On the one hand, there always seem to be people wanting to impose rules and regulations for Christians to follow. On the other hand, there have always been Christians who seem not to care about how they live, and who regard God's forgiveness as a blank cheque. How can we avoid these problems and be motivated to live a life pleasing to God? In Paul's short letter to Titus, God reveals the path to true godliness. Titus is not a long letter, but it gives you a thorough working over. Authors: Phillip Jensen and Tony Payne. £1.95

Other products...

NO GUTS NO GLORY

Good youth work is about making disciples of Jesus. *No Guts No Glory* shows you how to build a youth group that actually works towards this aim. You will learn how to set some goals for your group and how to reach those goals. Plus you'll get plenty of clear, down-to-earth advice on topics like: designing a successful program; choosing and training leaders; how to produce a group of Billy Grahams; relating to parents; making the most of games; discipline; how to run successful camps; sex in your youth group.

No Guts No Glory is full of lively illustrations, humour, practical advice and questions for discussion. An ideal basis for regular youth leader's meetings. Authors: Ken Moser, Alan Stewart and Edward Vaughan. £3.95

2 WAYS TO LIVE TRAINING COURSE

2 Ways to Live is a simple, 6-point Gospel presentation that is learnt by rote and then adapted to individual speech patterns and personalities. The training course guides trainees through this process as well as teaching valuable biblical principles of evangelism and dealing with some of the practical problems that we all face.

PERSONAL FOLLOW-UP TRAINING COURSE

Paul's relationship with the Thessalonian Christians is a model for personal follow-up. The *Personal Follow-up Course* aims to train Christians in this model.

Through group discussion, home study, and practical experience, trainees will learn how to build relationships with new or immature Christians and establish them in the faith. Trainees become familiar with seven basic Bible studies (called *Just for Starters*) and learn how to use these as a framework for personal follow-up. Topics include: God's offer of Salvation, My Response to God, Living by the Spirit, The Scriptures, Praye and Church.

FELLOW WORKERS

Church committees play a vital role in the spread of the Gospel in our society. They make many of the nuts-and-bolts decisions affecting ministry in the local congregation, and usually with very little outside support or input. Committee members are often keen to support the pastor (and his team), but sometimes are not sure where to start.

This set of discussion papers provide the stimulation, input and ideas that your church leadership needs—an excellent basis for discussion about where you're heading as a church. Authors: Phillip Jensen and Tony Payne. £3.50

THE BRIEFING

Read any good books lately? Or do all your reading projects stay on the shelf with bits of paper sticking out about a sixth of the way through?

In today's hectic world it's hard to find time to read books, but the need for stimulation and thought about how we should live as Evangelical Christians has never been greater. *The Briefing* provides the answer. You'll get 22 issues per year of short, sharp, thought-provoking comment and information You'll be stimulated, challenged and sometimes outraged—but you'll be thinking in an informed way.